# Christ in Genesis

## by Steven Teske

2017

Table of Contents

## Introduction

The entire Bible, from beginning to end, is about Jesus. People read and study the Bible for other reasons, but the primary reason God gave us the Bible was to teach us about our Redeemer. Whenever we read the Bible, no matter which part of it we are reading, we should expect to encounter Jesus.

This collection of essays, "Christ in Genesis," shows how our Redeemer can be found in the first book of the Bible. Some people read Genesis seeking only historical information about the past. The historic information it contains is accurate, but as a world history it is incomplete. Many important nations and empires are lumped together as "the nations" or encompassed as "the ends of the earth." Some people read Genesis seeking only literature. The book of Genesis contains fine literature which can be studied in the usual way. When people say that the Bible is more than literature, they (usually) do not mean that it is less than literature. Some people read Genesis looking for moral lessons about the commands of God and the consequences of obeying or disobeying those commands. Those lessons can be found and they are useful for correcting and rebuking sinners, but even they are not the central message of Genesis. Like every part of the Bible, the book of Genesis was written that we may know Jesus and, believing in him, receive eternal life (John 20:31).

Before beginning a book, though, the words in its title must be defined. By "Christ," I mean the Son of God, equal to God the Father in power and glory, wisdom and holiness—eternal, unchanging, and present everywhere in the universe. The same Christ is human, completely like every other human being, except that he never sinned. He was born at a certain time and place, he grew from a baby into a boy and then into a man, and he faced every temptation that is common to all people. He fell into the power of his enemies and was tortured and killed. The same weekend that he died, though, he rose from the dead to prove himself to be God's Son, the world's Redeemer, and Victor over evil in all its forms. He rules the universe today and will return on a Day known only to God, when he will judge all people and inaugurate a new and eternal world, a restoration of God's perfect creation.

By "Genesis," I mean the first book of the Hebrew Bible, which is also the first book of the Christian Old Testament. Moses is traditionally considered to be the author of five books, Genesis through Deuteronomy; this tradition was affirmed by Jesus (Mark 12:26, for example). Originally written in Hebrew, the book of Genesis has been translated into other languages, including a number of English translations. In these essays, Scripture quotations are from the Holy Bible, English Standard Version, © 2001 by Crossway Bibles, a division of Good News Publishers. Used by permission. All rights reserved.

This collection of essays is not intended to be a comprehensive commentary on the book of Genesis. I will not be dealing with difficult questions such as the meaning of "day" in the first chapter of Genesis. I will be skipping entire chapters which are significant to the accounts of the book of Genesis but less relevant to my chosen theme. I do not plan to address alternate theories about the authorship of Genesis or the context in which it was created.

Perhaps the most significant word in the title, though, is the word "in." Translators and interpreters of the Bible—or of any significant texts—find that the proper understanding of prepositions is a challenging but necessary skill. When I say that Christ is in Genesis, I mean that he is present in three significant ways.

First, the promise of his coming and of his messianic mission of redemption appears several times in Genesis. A promise is clearly stated before Adam and Eve after they have confessed their sin—this promise will later be fulfilled by Christ. God makes a promise to Abraham and repeats it to Isaac and to Jacob—

this promise also will be fulfilled by Christ. Jacob foresees a Redeemer and King coming from the family of Judah–this promise likewise will be fulfilled by Christ.

Christ is also present in Genesis as the eternal, unchanging, and omnipresent Son of God. Many interpreters of Genesis speak of a preincarnate Christ. They mean that Jesus was present in a human form but not as a human being, since he had not yet been conceived by the power of the Holy Spirit and born of the virgin Mary. They forget that Jesus Christ is the same yesterday, today, and forever (Hebrews 13:8). According to Paul's letter to the Ephesians, at the time of his ascension Jesus filled the universe in every way (Ephesians 4:10). This means that he fills time as well as space. In other words, the human body of Jesus traveled backward in time to wrestle Jacob, to eat with Abraham, and even to form Adam's body in the Garden of Eden. From his point of view, of course, Jesus did not travel through time, since he is present in every time and in every place. From our point of view, though, we can say that the human body of Jesus traveled through time.

John writes, "No one has ever seen God [the Father]; the only God, who is at the Father's side, he has made him known" (John 1:18). From this I conclude that every contact a person had with God as described in the Old Testament was contact with Jesus. Several books in the Old Testament mention the LORD (in Hebrew, Yahweh or Jehovah), the Angel of the LORD, and the Spirit of the LORD. As the Spirit of the LORD is easily recognized as God the Holy Spirit, so the Angel of the LORD is Jesus Christ, the Son of God, who has made the LORD known to his people.

Christ is found in Genesis in a third way. Many of the events recorded in the book of Genesis depict the work that Jesus would do to redeem sinners. I am not suggesting that the events in Genesis are not historically true; I am saying that these events are also pictures of Christ. In some cases, New Testament writings connect people and events from Genesis with Christ. In other cases, Christians from ancient times or from more recent times have noticed the connections. To avoid confusion, I am not using technical terms to describe these pictures or connections. However I am convinced that these pictures and connections are helpful to believers who know how Christ fulfilled the promises of the Old Testament, and also that they were helpful to believers who lived before Christ was born and who were still expecting the promised Redeemer.

Every part of the Bible is about Jesus. This is as true of the book of Genesis as it is true of the Gospels or the Epistles of the New Testament. Readers who encounter Christ in Genesis will better understand what is said of him in the Gospels and Epistles. The marvelous way in which Scripture interprets Scripture–the more difficult portions of the Bible being explained by the clearer passages–allows Christians to see Christ in Genesis in a way that nonbelievers are unlikely to perceive.

## In the Beginning

"In the beginning, God created the heavens and the earth" (Genesis 1:1). Traditionally, Christians think of God the Father as the Creator—"I believe in God the Father Almighty, Maker of heaven and earth" (The Apostles' Creed). Yet Genesis 1:2 tells us that "the Spirit of God was hovering over the waters."

The LORD was present. The Spirit of the LORD was present. What of the Angel of the LORD? We know from the New Testament that he was also present. "All things were made through him. Without him nothing was made that has been made" (John 1:2-3); "He is the image of the invisible God, the firstborn of all creation. For by him all things were created, in heaven and on earth, visible and invisible, whether thrones or dominions or rulers or authorities— all things were created through him and for him. And he is before all things, and in him all things hold together" (Colossians 1:15-17). He is called the firstborn, not because he came into being in time—for the Son of God is eternal, without beginning or ending, and unchanging—but because the Father has granted him all authority in heaven and on earth (Matthew 28:19). Because "all things were created through him and for him," we can think of creation as a gift of love which God the Father made for his Son.

John's Gospel refers to Jesus as the Word: "In the beginning, the Word was with God and the Word was God" (John 1:1). John chose the Greek word "logos," which had a special meaning to some Roman philosophers. They thought of the "logos" as an all-pervading principle of the universe—not a god, but in some ways greater than all the Roman gods.

Chinese philosophers describe the Dao in similar terms: "Dao can be talked about, but not the eternal Dao. Names can be named, but not the eternal Name. As the origin of heaven and earth, it is nameless; as the Mother of all things, it is nameable….Continually the Unnameable

13

moves on until it returns beyond the realm of things. We call it the formless Form, the imageless Image. We call it the indefinable and unimaginable. Confront it, and you do not see its face. Follow it, and you do not see its back. Yet, equipped with this timeless Dao, you can harness present realities. To know the origins is initiation into the Dao…. There was something undefined and yet complete in itself, born before heaven and earth. Silent and boundless, standing alone without change, yet pervading all without fail, it may be regarded as the Mother of the world. I do not know its name; I style it Dao; and, in the absence of a better word, call it the Great " (Daodejing 1, 14, and 25).

But "logos," meaning Word, reminds us also how God created. He spoke things into being. He said, "Let there be light," and there was light. God is all-powerful. He cannot lie, not simply because he is too good to lie, but because everything he says happens.

14

(Therefore, when God says, "you are forgiven," you can be certain that you are truly forgiven.) Jesus is the Word of God, the agent through whom all things were created. Yet he is not an impersonal logos or Dao; "The Word became flesh and made his dwelling among us" (John 1:14).

Creation was formless and empty when God first created it. In three days, the formless became formed. First, God said, "Let there be light," creating both energy and matter (for, as we know, matter can be converted into energy and vice versa, as Albert Einstein first described) as well as time and space (for those cannot exist apart from energy and matter). Then he separated the waters above from the waters below, and afterward he caused dry land to rise out of the water and covered it with vegetation.

After three days creation was formed, but it was still empty. God filled the light of the universe, creating the sun and all the other stars, the moon, and everything else in the vastness of the universe that emits light or reflects light. Next he filled the sky with flying creatures and the waters below with swimming creatures. Finally, he filled the land with walking and crawling creatures. As a culmination of all this creation, God made the first man and the first women. Six times, while he was creating, God described his creation as "good." When he had made the first man and the first woman, he changed his description to "very good."

Douglas Adams wrote, "In the beginning the Universe was created. This has made a lot of people very angry and has been widely regarded as a bad move" (*The Restaurant at the End of the Universe*).  Some religious movements, such as the Gnostics, agree that the physical world is bad. Genesis says that creation is good—and that, with human beings living in it, creation is very good. The source of evil comes after creation, but at its core, creation is good. Therefore, on the Day of the Lord, creation will be restored, complete with everything that was good when God first made it. Lions and wolves and lambs and oxen and even snakes are described in the new creation (Isaiah 11:6-9); I am sure that dogs and cats and goldfish will be there as well.

The first man and the first woman were both made in the image of God. Some people imagine this phrase to imply a recursion, in which the body of Jesus was the model for Adam's body, but then Jesus was born with such a body because he inherited from Adam's lineage. However, God said "let us make," suggesting that the image of God is the image of all three Persons, not just of the Son of God, the Word who became flesh. What then is the image of God? Several suggestions can be made. God is creative, and human beings also create. God is good, and human beings were created to be good. God is wise and all-knowing, and human beings are created to seek wisdom and knowledge. God is holy, and human beings also are meant to be holy.

Many adjectives describe God, including creative, good, wise, all-knowing, and holy. However, the Bible says that "God is love" (I John 4:8). God is not creation, or goodness, or knowledge, or holiness. Nor is God power or glory. He possesses all these things, but "God is love." Love is the very nature of God. The Father loves the Son and the Spirit. The Son loves the Father and the Spirit. The Spirit loves the Father and the Son. Had God created nothing, love would still be the very nature of God. Therefore, human beings were created for love. We were created to love God and to love each other. We were created to do good things for the glory of God and for the good of one another (Ephesians 2:10). When Jesus became flesh and lived among us, he showed us the image of God by loving his Father perfectly and bringing glory to him. He showed us the image of God by loving the people around them and serving them for their benefit.

When God said, "Let there be light," he knew each of us by name. He knew how we could glorify him and help each other, each with a unique set of abilities and resources and opportunities. He knew how we would fail to love, fail to glory, and fail to help. He knew the price he would have to pay to redeem us. When God rested, while creation was still very good, he knew that his rest prefigured the Sabbath when Jesus would rest—his body in a tomb, his spirit in the hands of his Father.

Yet, knowing all these things, God decided that creation was worthwhile. He loved us enough—in spite of everything he knew about us—to create the heavens and the earth, to begin the process that would bring the Son of God into the world to suffer and die for sinners, and to move toward the new creation where once again everything will be very good. God knew about you, and he said you were worth the trouble of creation and of redemption.

Therefore, God spoke the Word by whom all things were made.

In the garden

In the first chapter of Genesis, God creates everything in the universe by the power of his Word. In the second chapter of Genesis, God gets himself dirty, interacting directly with the materials he had created. Critics have noticed this and other differences between the two chapters and have suggested that the accounts contradict each other. Conspiracy theorists have said that the two accounts developed in different parts of Israel and were stuck together by an editor long after the time of Moses. The presence of Christ in Genesis provides a more satisfying explanation for the differences between these chapters.

Chapter one describes the Creator as God (Elohim). God creates the world by speaking; creation is accomplished through his Word and for his Word. Chapter two describes the Creator as the LORD God (Yahweh Elohim). The personal name of God indicates his personal involvement in creation. When God is this personally active in the world, we can be sure that Christ is at work. While the Father speaks, the Son gets dirty fulfilling his Father's will. This happens again in the Incarnation of Christ, when he is born and placed in a manger and spends more than thirty years among sinners, including some who reject him and execute him.

The order of creation appears to vary between the chapters. Chapter one presents a clear order of events, organized over six days. Plants were created on the third day, and land animals--including the first man and the first woman--were created on the sixth day. But in chapter two, the order of creation appears to be the man first, then plants, then animals, and finally the woman. The plants that are mentioned, though, are specifically garden plants. God created a garden after making the first man; he had already created vegetation earlier. Mention of the animals after the creation of the man but before the creation of the woman does not mean that God created in that order. The Hebrew language has only two tenses and uses them in various ways. The best translation of verse 19 is that "the LORD God had formed the animals" before making the man, and that after the man was formed and the garden planted, the LORD God brought the animals to the man.

Genesis 1:24 quotes God as saying, "Let the earth bring forth living creatures." Christ, the Word of God, responds by forming animals from the earth, as described in Genesis 2:19. Then he formed the body of Adam. I suggested earlier that the body of Christ as experienced in Genesis is the same body that was born in Bethlehem, that walked the dusty roads of Galilee and Judea, that was beaten, crucified, and buried, that rose on the third day and later ascended to fill the universe in both space and time. If I am correct about that body, then the hands which shaped the body of Adam were already scarred from the nails that held him to the cross.

After forming Adam from the earth, God 'breathed into his nostrils the breath of life." The same Hebrew word (ruach) can mean breath, wind, or spirit. Frequently the Bible makes use of this pun, as on Pentecost when the Holy Spirit announces his presence with the sound of a rushing wind. At the beginning of creation the Spirit of God was hovering over the waters. Here he is mentioned again as the instrument by which Adam receives life.

God brought every animal to Adam so that Adam would name them. To assign a name is to exercise authority. As in chapter one, authority to care for the planet and for its living beings is assigned to humanity. God had a second purpose for bringing the animals to Adam. He was preparing Adam for a special companion by first giving him the desire for a teammate with whom he could share his world and his authority.

"It is not good for the man to be alone," God said. Does God know how it feels to be alone? Outside of space and time, God is eternally three Persons: the Father, the Son, and the Holy Spirit. In a sense, then, God has never been alone--except for one occasion when the Son of God was truly alone. Hanging on the cross, atoning for the sins of the world, Jesus was forsaken by his Father. For a few hours, the Son of God was truly alone.

Jesus endured the torture of the cross, including the rejection of his Father, to redeem his people. He paid in full for the sins of the world so he could build a Church and claim a Bride. Paul wrote that every marriage is a picture of Christ and his Church. This surely must be true of the first marriage. To provide a bride for Adam, God had Adam fall into a deep sleep. To claim his Bride, Jesus fell into the sleep of death. After Jesus had died, a soldier prodded him with a spear, opening a wound in his side from which blood and water flowed. Medically this certifies that Jesus truly had died, since fluid had accumulated in his chest around his heart and lungs. In matters of faith, it also pictures the Bride of Christ, the Church, coming from the crucified Savior--water reminding us of Baptism and blood reminding us of the Lord's Supper, both important events in the life of the Church. And both Adam's sleep and Christ's sleep happened on a Friday, the sixth day of the week.

Eve was taken from Adam's side. Someone has said—it's attributed to various people--that she was not taken from Adam's head to rule him, nor from his foot to be trampled by him, but from his side to be next to him, from under his arm to be protected by him, and from near his heart to be loved by him. They were a team, both created in the image of God, both given authority over the planet and its living beings.

All this happened in a garden. The theme of gardens and wilderness runs through the Bible. Israel was promised a land flowing with milk and honey; but before they arrived in the Promised Land, they wandered in the wilderness for forty years. Jesus battled temptation in the wilderness. He was arrested in a garden and forced out of the garden, as Adam and Eve were sent out of the garden after their sin. Yet when he had won the war against evil, he was buried in a garden. In that garden, the news of his resurrection was first announced. The last two chapters of the Bible (Revelation 21-22) describe the new creation which will be our home after Jesus reveals his glory and announces his judgment. That description of the new creation signifies that our home, once again, will be a garden.

## A Tale of Two Trees

The Garden of Eden included an orchard of fruit-bearing trees. Perhaps there were apples, oranges, cherries, or mangoes--the Bible doesn't say. The only trees it names are the Tree of Life and the Tree of the Knowledge of Good and Evil.

Evidently the fruit of the Tree of Life provided its eater with unending life. I am not a biochemist and cannot explain how it did that; but, after their sin, Adam and Eve were barred from the Garden so they would not eat from the Tree of Life and live forever. Although this ban seems like a punishment, it actually was a blessing. Living forever as sinners in a sin-polluted world would not have been heavenly; it would have been the opposite of heaven. By making death available to Adam and Eve and to their descendants, the Lord is able to lead his people through the valley of death and beyond it to the house of the Lord--a new creation unstained by sin and evil.

The notorious Tree of the Knowledge of Good and Evil was named in retrospect. It had no magical ability to impart knowledge; the Bible does not say what purpose God had for this tree. Whatever its purpose was, it was not yet ready, so God told Adam and Eve not to eat the fruit of that tree. To suggest that God was testing Adam and Eve, wanting to know if they would obey him, is ludicrous. God knows all things; being timeless, he has already seen the future. Moreover, God does not tempt people to sin. The tree was created for a good reason, but we have not been told what that reason is.

Other writers have compared the Tree of the Knowledge of Good and Evil to a large pot of soup being heated on the stove. Mother tells her three-year-old son, "Don't touch the pot, or you'll be burned." Against her warning, he touches the pot, spilling its contents upon himself, and he is burned. In fact, he is so badly burned that she must rush him to the hospital for treatment. She did not heat the pot to test his obedience; she was making lunch for the family. At the hospital, though, she does not explain that to him. Treatment for his burns is more important than explanations. In the same way, when Adam and Eve ate the forbidden fruit, we all got burned. God has provided a way to be healed, but he has not told us why the tree was in the Garden.

Trees, like gardens, are frequently mentioned in the Bible. Deuteronomy 21:22-23 proclaims a curse on anyone who dies hanging from a tree. The first Psalm compares a righteous man to a fruitful tree. A rebellious son of David was killed while hanging from a tree. Zacchaeus climbed a tree to see Jesus, but Jesus called him out of the tree. Jesus was going to hang on the tree of the cross, receiving the curse deserved by sinners, dying to grant eternal life to his people. He called Zacchaeus out of the tree because he-- the ultimate Son of David--would go to a tree for Zacchaeus.

Jesus wants his people to bear good fruit. His orchard is filled with trees, but by ourselves we bear no good fruit. We have sinned, doing what we should not do, and failing to perform the good works we were created to do. Of all the trees in the orchard, only one tree bears good fruit. That tree is Jesus Christ. This one fruitful tree accepted the curse of the barren trees to reverse the condition of the orchard. Now all the trees in the orchard bear good fruit except for one dead tree in the middle of the orchard-- Christ's cross.

His cross is our tree of life. Through the cross where Christ suffered and died, we receive eternal life. Because he has given us life, we are now able to bear fruit; we are able to become the people God intended when he created us.

Jesus once told a parable about a fruitless tree. The landowner was prepared to remove the tree and change it into firewood. The gardener asked for one more year; he offered to prepare the ground around the tree with the hope that it would bear fruit (Luke 13:6-9). Each of us is that tree, and Jesus is the Gardener who pleads for us. He does all the work necessary to make us able to bear fruit so we will not be thrown into the fire. Instead of the fire, our future home is the garden of the new creation. According to Revelation 22:2, the Tree of Life will be available to us there, ensuring that we will live forever.

## Forbidden fruit and fig leaves

Adam and Eve ate the forbidden fruit,
disobeying God's command and bringing sin,
evil, and death into his creation. Their first sin
did not happen when their teeth touched the
fruit and they bit and chewed and swallowed.
Their first sin did not happen when one of them
reached out a hand to pick the fruit. Their first
sin was the decision to doubt God's word, to
believe that he had been less than truthful with
them, and to test him by breaking his
commandment.

Genesis describes the tempter as a serpent.
Revelation 12:9 gives us his full identity: "the
great dragon was thrown down, that ancient
serpent, who is called the devil and Satan, the
deceiver of the whole world." Satan was one of
the good angels God had created, but through
pride he rebelled against God. A Muslim
tradition states that Satan rebelled when God
told him to worship and serve Adam. I suspect
that the devil's pride and arrogance are the

33

result of a lack of understanding. He has contempt for the love of God. He understands power and authority, but not love. He thinks that he can run the universe better than God is running it, so he is trying to take authority over creation. One of his first acts of rebellion was to invite Adam and Eve to join his rebellion.

God had commanded Adam and Eve to do several things: to be fruitful and multiply, to care for the earth and its living creatures, and to rest every seventh day as God had rested on the seventh day. Any of these commands was an opportunity for a temptation to disobey God. Satan chose the fruit as the easiest way to challenge Eve's faithfulness to God's commands. His suggestion that God had forbidden them to eat from any tree in the Garden seems ludicrous, but it shows his usual procedure. He wants to make God seem overbearing and unloving. By twisting God's commands, Satan hopes to inspire resentment and rebellion in our minds.

The devil misquoted God's command. He showed that he knew exactly what God had said—when Eve said, "lest we die," Satan responded, "You will not surely die." Even as he calls God a liar, Satan corrects Eve's recollection of what God had said. Of course they did not physically die the day they ate the fruit; Adam lived another 930 years. There are worse things than physical death. Spiritual death is separation from God. Adam and Eve spiritually died with their first sin. Whoever is spiritually dead when he or she physically dies will be eternally dead. Whoever is spiritually alive when he or she physically dies will have eternal life. Jesus experienced spiritual death on the cross when he was forsaken by his Father; he went there so that Adam and Eve and each of their descendants would not have to go there.

Satan persuaded Eve that eating the forbidden fruit would make her and Adam more like God. They had already been created in God's image. There was no way for them to become more like God. Eve saw that the tree was good for fruit and pleasing to the eyes. Believing that it would also make her wise, she ate and she gave some fruit to Adam and he ate. Being separated from God by their sin, they observed their nakedness and were ashamed. Therefore, they made loincloths for themselves from fig leaves.

A fig leaf loincloth will not last very long. The leaves quickly wither and crumble, leaving the maker naked again. All our efforts to fix our own lives are equally futile. We cannot hide our sins from God, even if we think we have hidden them from ourselves.

After God had confronted them about their sin, he also provided for them. In place of their fig leaf loincloths, God gave them garments of animal skins. The clothing that God provided was more useful than what Adam and Eve made for themselves. However, this gift from God meant that some of the animals Adam and Eve had known now were dead, just to provide them with clothing. Physical death was made real to them in this way, now that they had experienced spiritual death. The animals gave their lives to clothe Adam and Eve for their protection and for the sake of decency.

These animals that died are images of Jesus, who would also die to cover our sins. We are clothed in his righteousness, which makes us acceptable in the sight of God and protects us from evil. Throughout the Bible, clothing takes special significance, picturing a life that is pleasing to God. Jesus was stripped of his clothing on the day he died; it was claimed by the soldiers who executed him. Yet Jesus has also clothed us, surrendering his life so we could inherit his righteousness.

## Confession and promise

"And they heard the sound of the LORD God walking in the garden in the cool of the day..." This sounds so pleasant, Jesus taking a walk in the garden. (How do we know it was Jesus? "No one has ever seen God [the Father]; the only God, who is at the Father's side, he has made him known"--John 1:18.) I don't know the history of the translation of this verse, but the original Hebrew has a different tone. The word translated "cool" is ruach, the same word that means breath or wind or spirit; and I do not think "cool" is used to translate this word anywhere else in the Bible. In the first Greek translation of Genesis (in the Septuagint), the translators chose to render the word "fear." Jesus approached Adam and Eve in the spirit of the Day--that is, the Day of the Lord, the Day of God's wrath at sin, Judgment Day.

No wonder Adam and Eve tried to hide from Jesus. They had sinned, dying spiritually, rebelling against God. They were guilty. They were ashamed. They tried to cover their shame with fig leaves, but human works cannot cover our sins. Jesus called them: "Where are you?" When Adam confessed his shame, Jesus asked him, "Did you eat the fruit I told you not to eat?"

The Lord gave Adam and Eve an opportunity to confess their sin--to repent. The topic of repentance can be confusing. On the one hand, God wants us to repent and calls upon us to repent. On the other hand, nothing we do earns God's forgiveness. There is nothing you have to do for God to forgive your sins. The best resolution of this seeming contradiction is to know that, when God commands us to repent, he also gives us the ability to repent. (Compare this to Jesus telling a lame man to walk, or telling a dead man to come out of his tomb.) Repentance (like faith) is something God does in us, not something we do for God.

Adam tries a sly sort of repentance. He says, "The woman whom you gave to be with me, she gave me the fruit of the tree, and I ate." He points a finger of blame at Eve, and subtly even tries to blame God. ("If you hadn't made this woman, we wouldn't have this problem.") If Adam had been thinking more quickly, he might have added, "She gave me fruit from the tree you made. Why did you make it if you didn't want us to eat it?" Many of Adam's descendants have tried the same sort of escape from guilt, blaming God for making sin possible.

When God questions Eve, she shows herself to be a quick learner. She also points a finger of blame, this time at the snake. "The serpent deceived me, and I ate."

The poor serpent has no fingers to point, and Jesus does not give him the opportunity to make excuses. Knowing that the serpent is Satan in disguise, Jesus essentially says, "You chose that form for your rebellion--now accept the consequences. You are going to crawl on the ground. You are going to eat dust." In other words, "You are the loser in this contest."

Jesus adds that there will be enmity between the woman and Satan and between their offspring. This means more than the idea that women generally fear snakes. It means that the devil did not gain allies in his rebellion against God. He merely broadened the battlefield. When the key battle in the war between God and evil would be fought, a descendant of Eve would win, and the devil would lose.

"He shall bruise your head." Those words promise victory over Satan. "You shall bruise his heel." Those words speak of the pain the Savior must bear while defeating the devil. The cross of Christ is described with these words. God is addressing the snake, but his message is for Adam and Eve. Through their descendant, God will win the war against evil, reversing the consequences of their sin. God's words to the snake are the first preaching of the Gospel.

Meanwhile, the consequences of their sin remain. Family relationships are distorted because of sin. Work in the world is hard labor (whether physical or mental, whether challenging or boring) because of sin. Physical death is a consequence of sin. Jesus created Adam from dirt. Through physical death, Adam will return to the dirt. The ground itself is cursed because of the sin of Adam and Eve.

Yet, as God curses the snake and curses the ground, he does not curse Adam and Eve. He has promised victory through the cross; even the promise itself reverses the curse of sin. Adam and Eve did not have to wait for Christ to be born, to suffer, to die, and to rise again, before they could be spiritually alive again. Believing the promise of the coming Savior and the coming victory, they were already given saving faith. Even though their bodies would die, they already had eternal life.

## Raising Cain, raising Abel

Because of their sin, Adam and Eve were removed from the Garden of Eden and were not allowed to return. Yet they left with a promise that they would be rescued by a descendant of Eve who would crush the serpent's head and would reconcile them to God. Adam and Eve's children faced the same burden of sin that their parents had brought into the world, but they also inherited the same promise of forgiveness and reconciliation.

When Eve gave birth to her firstborn, a son, she uttered a sentence which consists, in Hebrew, of three words: "I-have-gotten, a-man, the-LORD." Most translations add helping words to her sentence, rendering it as, "I have gotten a man with the help of the LORD." Even the Septuagint, the Hebrew Bible translated into Greek more than twenty-two centuries ago, adds the proposition "apo," meaning "from," in front of the Name of the Lord. A few Bible scholars believe that adding words to this sentence is a mistake. For example, Martin Luther taught that Eve had said, "I have gotten a man, the LORD." Luther believed that Eve understood the promise of her descendant, who would crush the devil's head, would be God taking on human form, as Jesus took on human form from his mother, Mary. If indeed Eve thought that her firstborn son was the promised Savior, what a dreadful disappointment occurred when Cain instead became history's first murderer.

When they had grown to manhood, Cain and his brother Abel both offered sacrifices to the Lord. God accepted the sacrifice of Abel but rejected the sacrifice of Cain. Much needless speculation has tried to discover the difference between the two sacrifices. The answer is found in Hebrews 11:4. Abel offered an acceptable sacrifice "by faith." Cain evidently did not offer his sacrifice by faith. No sacrifice to God has any value if it is not offered by faith.

All the animal sacrifices of the Old Testament were pictures of Jesus suffering and dying on the cross, having his heal bruised as he crushed the head of the serpent. No sacrifice, other than Christ, ever purchased mercy and forgiveness from God. No human act, other than the work of Christ, can purchase God's forgiveness. God hates the times when people go through the motions of worship or sacrifice apart from faith in him. (See Isaiah 1:14, Amos 5:21-23, and Psalm 50:7-11.) He wants these things to be done by faith. When people do these things without thinking about what they mean, God is displeased. When people do these things thinking that they are earning something from God, putting him in debt to them, God is angered.

The animals that died so Adam and Eve could be clothed were pictures of Jesus. Likewise, the firstborn animal offered by Abel—and the countless animals offered to God by his people over the centuries—were pictures of Jesus. It appears that Cain forgot this important truth. He offered a sacrifice to God, but not by faith. Therefore God did not accept the sacrifice Cain offered. The fact that Cain was angry to have his sacrifice refused shows that he expected to gain something from God by that sacrifice.

Jesus warned Cain of the dangerous temptation lurking in his anger. Cain ignored the warning. Instead, he acted in violence, murdering his brother. He thought that his crime would be secret, but no one keeps secrets from God. As God had given Adam and Eve the opportunity to confess their sin, so Jesus also asked Cain about Abel.

Cain lied to God. He said that he did not know where Abel was. "Am I my brother's keeper?" Cain asked. The answer to that question is "yes." We are all commanded to love our neighbors as ourselves, and a brother is a very near neighbor. We are all expected to help one another, to bear each other's burdens. Obeying God's commandment not to murder is not as simple as never violently taking another's life. We are not to hurt or harm our neighbors, but we are to help them and care for them. Neglecting a neighbor in his or her need is sinful, just as violently striking him or her is sinful.

Jesus challenged Cain's lie. "The voice of your brother's blood is crying to me from the ground," Jesus said. Other Bible verses also describe the blood of victims as crying for justice. Because God loves each of us, God is angry when any of us are hurt by a fellow human being. All the blood of all victims in history cries for justice, and God hears those cries. On the Day of the Lord, the justice of God will be revealed. Those who have harmed their neighbors will finally receive what they deserve.

Cain knew what he deserved. He had taken away his brother's life; now he deserved to be killed. His parents, his other brothers and sisters, his nephews and nieces all had the right to take vengeance on the killer of Abel. Yet God did not give Cain what Cain deserved. Instead, Cain was marked by God so that no one would kill him, even though he deserved to be killed.

The firstborn animal offered by Abel was a picture of Jesus. Abel himself became a picture of Jesus, innocent before God and yet killed by his brother. Jesus was rejected by his own people and sent to his death. Yet the blood of Jesus does not cry for vengeance. Instead, in his death, Jesus prays, "Father, forgive them." His blood is more powerful than the blood of Abel. Our sins caused the suffering and death of Jesus, but now he washes us in his blood to redeem us as God's people. Because of the death of Jesus, we will not receive what we deserve on the Day of the Lord. Instead, we will receive what Jesus deserves—eternal life in God's perfect new creation.

Like Cain, we have been marked by God so we will not receive what we deserve. He has marked us with the blood of Christ; he has marked us with his own Holy Spirit. On the Last

Day, Jesus will see that mark on us and claim us as his people. He has already paid to purchase us. Now and forever we belong to him.

## Noah, the Ark, and the Flood

Noah, the ark, and the Flood are familiar to almost every person living in western culture. Efforts to recreate this account for movies inevitably bring new details into the story; the description in the Bible does not provide nearly enough material for a feature-length movie. Many people probably think that they know about Noah, the ark, and the Flood, but much of what they know might be fiction that has been added to the Bible's account.

Noah is easily seen as a picture of Jesus. Noah is a savior, obeying the commands of God and—through his obedience—rescuing and preserving lives from God's wrath and judgment. From the time Noah began building the ark until the time rain began to fall, 120 years passed, according to the usual understanding of Genesis 6:3. During this time, by his words and by his actions, Noah was able to prepare his neighbors for the coming destruction, warning them to repent before it was too late. By the same token, Jesus spent about three years teaching in Galilee and Judea and the surrounding area, calling upon people to "repent and believe in the gospel" (Mark 1:15). The structure which Noah built to save lives was made of wood; the cross where Jesus suffered and died to bestow eternal life was also made of wood. Those who were to be saved entered the ark through an opening in its side, faintly echoing the Bride of Christ coming from his side as Eve came from the rib of Adam.

Those who accept the premise, based on John 1:18, that God the Father is revealed only through Jesus—and that, when God speaks or is seen in Genesis, Jesus is present among his people—will picture Jesus visiting Noah and giving him detailed instructions about how to build the ark. We are told that Noah was righteous and blameless, but we also know that only Jesus is without sin. Noah was made righteous and blameless through his faith in the promised Savior. All believers, from Adam and

Eve until the glorious appearing of Christ, are saved in the same way—by God's grace, through faith in Jesus.

Often the Flood is seen only as an act of wrath, God's judgment on a sinful world. The water of the Flood also had a cleansing action, washing away sinners and the consequences of their sins. The apostle Peter wrote about the time "when God's patience waited in the days of Noah, while the ark was being prepared, in which a few, that is, eight persons, were brought safely through water. Baptism, which corresponds to this, now saves you...." (I Peter 3:20-21). The water of the Flood lifted Noah and his family out of a sinful world and carried them safely in the ark until they landed in a new world, a world which had been washed clean by water. Likewise, Christians are carried through this sinful world by the work of Jesus and of the Holy Spirit until we land safely in the new world God has promised us—a world won for us by the work of Christ.

Peter stresses that eight persons were saved by the Flood and by the ark. He stresses this number, so it must be significant. God created the world in seven days, establishing the length of the week. Sets of seven in the Bible often represent completeness. The eighth day is the beginning of a new week. Holy Week begins on Palm Sunday and ends on the eighth day, Easter Sunday—the day that Jesus rose from the dead to demonstrate his victory over sin and death, the day that promises his people new life in a new creation. Like Peter, early Christian writers often associated the number eight with a new beginning, as they also associated Baptism with a new beginning. The apostle Paul wrote, "Do you not know that all of us who have been baptized into Christ Jesus were baptized into his death? We were buried therefore with him by Baptism into death, in order that, just as Christ was raised from the dead by the glory of the Father, we too might walk in newness of life" (Romans 6:3-4).

When Noah and his family exited the ark, Noah offered sacrifices to God, continuing the tradition of "pre-enacting" the sacrifice of Christ on the cross. Afterward, he planted a garden. This garden is no minor detail; it reinforces the concept of a new beginning, since Adam and Eve began in a garden. Yet, as Adam and Eve sinned and were driven from the garden, so Noah's garden also became his downfall. He drank wine, made from the grapes of his vineyard, became drunk, and lay naked, uncovered in his tent. In spite of his new beginning, Noah was no longer clothed in righteousness. One son laughed at Noah's nakedness, bringing trouble upon himself and his family. The other two sons covered Noah's nakedness, bringing blessing upon themselves and their families. In the same way, Christians today should not rejoice in the wrongdoing of others, but instead should seek to share the good news of Jesus with sinners, hoping to clothe them in his righteousness by the power of his Word. We do not desire to humiliate

54

them over their sins or condemn them, but we hope instead to call them to repentance and faith.

God promised Noah that he would never again flood the world to destroy it. He established the rainbow as a sign of that promise—a reminder to God of the promise he had made. Rainbows mean different things to different people today, but they remain to God a reminder of his mercy upon his creation. Light shines through the clouds, and through the drops of water they produce, to display a rainbow upon the earth. God's light comes through water to his people to display God's promise of new and eternal life for all those who trust his promises.

## The tower of Babel

Like the account of Noah, the account of the
Tower of Babel seems at first glance to indicate
nothing more than God's wrath and
punishment. Yet Christ is present even in this
short section of the Bible. We perceive the
wisdom of God's judgment, and we also pick up
a clue about the final reconciliation of the world
to God through Jesus Christ from this account.

The descendants of Noah gathered on the plain
of Shinar, which is now in modern Iraq. Here
they decided to bake bricks and build a city
which would include a tower with its top in the
heavens. These actions violated no specific
commands of God, nor does God frown on our
modern cities with their many towers and
skyscrapers. The purpose of the builders,
however, contradicted the will of God. They
said, "Let us make a name for ourselves, lest we
be dispersed over the face of the whole earth."
God had said, "You, be fruitful and multiply,

teem on the earth and multiply in it" (Genesis 9:7).

The people who wanted to make a name for themselves said, "Come, let us build." God said, "Come, let us go down." Father, Son, and Holy Spirit investigated the city and the tower and the hearts of the builders. God said, "Nothing they propose to do will now be impossible for them." In my opinion, this statement of God was meant as irony. He was echoing what the builders believed, not what God knew to be true.

God's response to their pride was to cause them to speak a variety of languages so they could no longer understand each other. Not only did each of them hear the others speaking other languages; each of them was convinced that he or she was speaking the right language while the others were speaking the wrong languages. Humble people learn how to communicate with one another in spite of language barriers. Proud people, even today, insist that they are speaking the right language and that other people should learn their language if they have anything to say to them. Because these people were proud, they were unable to work together. They abandoned the city and the tower and were dispersed over the face of the earth. This dispersal was exactly what God had wanted, and it was exactly what the builders had hoped to avoid.

Judgment and punishment are one answer to sin. Forgiveness and reconciliation are another answer to sin. God prefers the second answer. Therefore he sent his Son, the Word made flesh, to atone for sin and to reconcile the world to God. When the time was right, Jesus offered his body as a sacrifice. He died and was buried. On the third day he rose again from the dead. He spent time with his disciples, explaining what he had done and why. Then, forty days after his resurrection, he ascended into heaven to fill the universe in every way.

Fifty days after his resurrection, Jesus poured out the Holy Spirit on his Church. Everyone in the city heard the sound of a rushing wind—a signature event, since in the Biblical languages (Hebrew and Greek) the same word means both wind and spirit. Those who believed in Jesus were marked with tongues of fire. They began to talk about Jesus, and the various people from various parts of the world all heard the Christians sharing the good news of Jesus in different languages—each listener heard the Gospel in his or her own language.

With this miracle, God showed that sins were forgiven and reconciliation had happened. The results of sin—including the judgment which resulted in many languages—were reversed by the work of Jesus. God dispersed the many nations, but from those many nations he has assembled one Kingdom, which is the Holy Christian Church. In this Church, the work of Jesus and of the Holy Spirit continues to be accomplished all over the world. When God gathers his people, they come from every tribe and nation and language, united by one Savior and by one Holy Spirit.

The promise to Abraham

When Abraham is introduced in the book of Genesis, one of the first things we learn about him is that God has made him a promise. "Now the Lord said to Abram, 'Go from your country and your kindred and your father's house to the land that I will show you. And I will make of you a great nation, and I will bless you and make your name great, so that you will become a blessing. I will bless those who bless you, and him who dishonors you I will curse; and in you all the families of the earth shall be blessed'" (Genesis 12:1-3).

Abraham does not earn God's blessing by traveling to Canaan as God commanded. The blessing is a gift, unearned, and Abraham's journey is a result of the blessing, not a cause of the blessing. Over the years, God repeats his blessing to Abraham, also to Isaac, and to Jacob. He says it different ways on different occasions, but generally it comes in three parts: Abraham's family will become a great nation, they will live on the land to which God sent Abraham, and from that nation on that land will come a blessing for the entire world.

Abraham had to wait twenty-five years for a beginning to the first part of the blessing. Isaac was not born until Abraham was one hundred years old. Isaac did not marry for another forty years, and then he had two sons. His son Jacob had twelve sons and a daughter. The family had grown to seventy members by the time they moved to Egypt. When they left Egypt several generations later, the Israelites included 603,550 men of fighting age, as well as children, women, and the elderly.

They returned to the land God had promised to Abraham, Isaac, and Jacob; and land became a very important part of God's covenant with the Israelites. Each of the tribes of Israel was assigned a certain portion of land, carefully described in the book of Joshua—except the tribe of Levi was given no land. The Law of Moses ordered strict punishment upon anyone who tried to steal land by moving a boundary stone. Land could not be sold; families in debt could rent out use of their land for a time, but they would receive their land again at the next Jubilee Year, which came every fifty years.

Generally when the Romans conducted a census, they simply went door-to-door, counting the members of each household and collecting a tax. The Jews made this census more complicated than anyone else in the Empire. Joseph (and many others like him) was determined to be counted at his family's land rather than at his current residence; so Joseph took Mary his espoused wife and traveled from Nazareth in Galilee to Bethlehem in Judea, because Joseph was a descendant of King David. David had many other descendants who wanted to be counted in Bethlehem, so the inn (more of a guest room than a motel) was full, and Mary and Joseph had to take shelter in a cave, one that generally was used to shelter sheep. There Mary gave birth to her firstborn, the ultimate

Son of David, who was swaddled and placed in a manger. According to the Law of Moses and the prophecy of Micah, the Son of David was required to be born in Bethlehem to inherit his kingdom.

Jesus is, of course, the blessing for the entire word who came from the family of Abraham on the land that had been promised to Abraham. He was born to inherit a kingdom and to win a victory. His victory was not over King Herod or the Romans. His victory was over all the forces of evil, including sin and death. His kingdom was for all people, not just for the Jews. John the Baptist and Jesus and the apostle Paul all insisted that the children of Abraham are all those who share the faith of Abraham in God's promises, not necessarily those who can trace their family tree back to Abraham.

God affirmed his promise to Abraham several times. In Genesis 15 God commanded a ceremony involving several animals that were cut in half. I have read that this ceremony represented a form of covenant that was practiced in western Asia three to four thousand years ago. Generally two people making an agreement would walk between the halves of a slaughtered animal. In this case, Jesus walks alone (with a fire pot and a torch) between the halves, showing again that the fulfillment of the promise depended upon Jesus entirely and not upon Abraham in any way.

When Abraham was ninety-nine years old, God gave another ceremony to Abraham and to his family: the ceremony of circumcision. A small bit of skin was snipped away from the most vulnerable part of a man's body. Some pain was felt, and a little blood was shed. For the rest of his life, that man had a private reminder of his relationship with God. Babies born into the family, if they were male, were circumcised on the eighth day (the same day of the week that he had been born). Jesus was circumcised in this way, shedding a little blood to foreshadow the blood he would shed more than thirty years later in the battle that won the victory.

Abraham never owned any of the land where he lived, except for a cemetery he bought when his wife died. His descendants claimed that land under Joshua when they battled the Canaanites with the help of God. When they were unfaithful to God, they lost control of the land to Midianites and Philistines and other enemies. This was God's judgment upon his people for their sins. As their sins grew worse, God called the Assyrians and the Babylonians to remove the people from the land; but because of his promise of a blessing for the entire world, God called the Persians to send the Jews back to the Promised Land. God's Promise is always bigger than his Judgment.

God always keeps his promises. The accounts of Abraham and his family cannot be understood apart from an understanding of the promises of God.

## Melchizedek

In Genesis 14, Abraham leads a commando unit to rescue Lot and the other citizens of Sodom after they have been seized in a raid led by four kings from the east. Abraham's mission is successful, and afterward Abraham is blessed by Melchizedek, king of Salem and priest of God most high. Abraham gives Melchizedek a tenth of everything. The identity of Melchizedek is a puzzle. He is mentioned in Psalm 110 and plays a prominent role in the letter to the Hebrews, where Jesus is declared to be a priest in the order of Melchizedek.

Some people have suggested that Melchizedek is Jesus, the same Jesus who spoke with Abraham on many occasions and even ate at the tent of Abraham. Another suggestion is that Melchizedek is Shem, the son of Noah, who lived 502 years beyond the flood. (This is an interesting suggestion, as Methuselah, according to the book of Genesis, was born early enough to have known Adam and lived long enough to know Noah and his sons. Now Shem was born early enough to have known Methuselah and lived long enough to known Abraham.) Both these suggestions overlook an important truth: Abraham and his family were not the only people on earth who believed in God. Although the promise of salvation was being carried out through the family of Abraham, other people also believed that promise and were saved through the future work of Jesus. As a priest of God, Melchizedek taught and served some of those people.

Hebrews 7 notes that Melchizedek is a picture of Jesus. His name means "king of righteousness," and as king of Salem he is also "king of peace." Like Jesus, Melchizedek is both a king and a priest. This was forbidden in Israel. King Saul was rejected by God because as king he offered sacrifices to God rather than waiting for Samuel to arrive. King Uzziah was punished, stricken with leprosy, because he burned incense to the Lord in the Temple, which was intended only for priests to do (II Chronicles 26:16-21). In Israel, no one but Jesus Christ was fit to serve as both priest and king.

All the kings of Israel and Judah were pictures of Jesus, the King of kings and the Lord of lords. Jesus is the ultimate King, but every other king is a picture of Jesus. Even bad kings are bad pictures of Jesus. All the priests of Israel were pictures of Jesus, making offerings for the forgiveness of sins, representing the people to God and pleading for their forgiveness. Jesus is the ultimate Priest, offering himself as full payment for all the sins of history, pleading to his Father for our forgiveness. Even evil priests and ungodly sacrifices are bad pictures of Jesus. By combining these jobs, Melchizedek was a unique picture of Jesus. Only he and Jesus belong to the order which bears his name.

## Abraham, Father of Faith

Abraham is called the Father of Faith. The apostle Paul and the writer of the letter to the Hebrews both stress the faith of Abraham, the fact that he trusted God even when the son God had promised appeared increasingly unlikely every year. The two actions that demonstrate Abraham's faith are these: in obedience to God, he traveled to Canaan; and, in obedience to God, he prepared to offer his son Isaac as a burnt offering.

Between these two acts of faith, probably more than thirty years apart, Abraham often demonstrated the weakness of his faith. During a time of famine, Abraham left Canaan and traveled to Egypt, evidently doubting that God would take care of him during the famine. In Egypt, he persuaded Sarah to call herself his sister rather than his wife, evidently doubting that God would protect Abraham and his family in Egypt. Although he believed that God would provide him a son, he also tried to help God keep this promise. First, he suggested that he would adopt his servant Eliezer to produce a son for God. Later, he accepted Sarah's suggestion that her maid Hagar be a surrogate mother to produce a son for God. God had to insist to Abraham that neither Eliezer nor Ishmael (Abraham's son by Hagar) was the promised son. Then, in the land of Gerar, Abraham once more persuaded Sarah to say that she was his sister, not his wife, evidently still doubting that God would protect Abraham and his family from the power of King Abimelech.

One day Jesus and two angels were traveling towards Sodom, and they stopped at the tent of Abraham. Abraham recognized Jesus and insisted that the group stay for a meal. He ordered a calf slaughtered and fresh bread made, and Jesus and the angels enjoyed his hospitality. During the meal, Jesus told Abraham that by that time next year, Sarah would have a son. Sarah overheard the promise and laughed, but when Jesus asked why she was laughing she lied and said, "I didn't laugh."

After Jesus had sent the angels to Sodom, Jesus told Abraham that he was investigating Sodom and that he would destroy the city if things were as bad there as he had heard. Abraham knew how bad things were in Sodom, and so he began to bargain with God (always the sign of a weak faith). He had Jesus promise not to destroy Sodom if fifty righteous people were living there. Then, step by step, Abraham worked his way down to ten righteous people. Each time Jesus agreed, even though Jesus knew that not a single person in Sodom was righteous. Knowing the intention of Abraham's prayer, Jesus did something Abraham hadn't asked: he had the angels remove Lot and his family from the city before burning sulfur fell from the sky to destroy Sodom and the sinners who lived there.

Abraham's faith was weak, but it still was saving faith, because it was faith in the right God. Our faith can be as weak as Abraham's faith. We say we believe God's promises, and then we do things our way rather than his way. We say we believe his promises, and then we struggle to make them come true by our efforts. We say we believe his promises, and then we try to bargain with God instead of trusting that his will is good. Yet when we put our trust in God, even though our faith is weak, God saves us by his grace through faith. Abraham is our father because we are like him: clinging to Christ with a feeble faith, but saved all the same by the strength of Christ's work.

Miracle babies, and the rights of the firstborn

Some people say that every birth is a miracle.
To a certain extent, I suppose that is true. There
would be no babies, or flowers, or ears of corn,
if not for the God who made everything in the
beginning and who still provides for his creation
every day. But when everything is a miracle,
then nothing is miraculous. When a baby enters
the world in the usual way, we thank God for
the new life. When a baby enters the world in a
special way, we marvel at the miracle.

God told Abraham that his family would
become a mighty nation, but Abraham and
Sarah had no children. When God first spoke his
promise, Abraham was seventy-five years old,
and Sarah was sixty-five. As the years passed,
neither of them was getting any younger. Twice
Abraham tried to help God keep God's promise.
First, Abraham proposed to adopt Eliezer, his
chief servant, as his heir. Later, at Sarah's
suggestion, he used her servant Hagar as a
surrogate mother. Both times, God said no to

Abraham. The promised heir would be born from Sarah, in a manner that would be undoubtedly a miracle.

Sarah was ninety years old when Isaac was born. Only God could cause such a thing to happen. To underline the point, God repeated this miracle every few generations. Manoah's wife could have no children until Jesus appeared to her and promised a son, who was Samson, the mighty man of Israel. Hannah, the wife of Elkanah, could have no children until she prayed to the Lord for a son, who was Samuel, the last judge of Israel. Elisabeth, the wife of the priest Zechariah, was too old to have children, but Gabriel appeared to Zechariah and promised him a son, who was John the Baptist.

All these miracles happened to prepare God's people for a different kind of miracle. Isaiah told King Ahaz about the coming miracle: "Behold, the virgin shall conceive and bear a son, and shall call his name Emmanuel" (Isaiah 7:14). While it is true that the word translated "virgin" could simply mean "young woman" in Hebrew, it is also true that the word always designated an unmarried woman. Other words were appropriate for unmarried women who were not virgins. When the fullness of time had come, God sent forth his Son, born of a woman, born under the law, so we might receive adoption as sons (Galatians 4:4-5). Mary gave birth to her firstborn son and wrapped him in swaddling cloths and laid him in a manger, because there was no place for them in the inn (Luke 2:7).

Because Abraham did not trust God to keep God's promise without Abraham's help, Ishmael was born before Isaac. In Deuteronomy, it is written: "If a man has two wives, the one loved and the other unloved, and both the loved and the unloved have borne him children, and if the firstborn son belongs to the unloved, then on the day when he assigns his possessions as an inheritance to his sons, he may not treat the son of the loved as the firstborn in preference to the son of the unloved, who is the firstborn, but he shall acknowledge the firstborn, the son of the unloved, by giving him a double portion of all that he has, for he is the firstfruits of his strength. The right of the firstborn is his" (Deuteronomy 21:15-17). Clearly this was written long after Ishmael and Isaac were born, but many ancient civilizations had similar rules. A man's firstborn son was always to be his primary heir, receiving at least twice as much as any other son.

In Abraham's family, this rule is repeatedly broken. God favors Isaac over Ishmael, even when Abraham pleads for Ishmael, the firstborn son. God favors Jacob over Esau, even though Esau was born first. Jacob favors Joseph, the son of his favorite wife, over all of Joseph's brothers, most of whom were older than Joseph. Joseph even receives a double portion in his inheritance; instead one tribe of Joseph, there are two: the tribes of Ephraim and Manasseh. Meanwhile, the promise to

Abraham, Isaac, and Jacob is passed down to Judah, the fourth son of Jacob. When Jacob blesses Joseph's sons, he gives priority to Ephraim, even though Manasseh was Joseph's firstborn son.

How is Christ pictured by this anomaly? Jesus Christ is eternally the Son of God the Father; the rights of the firstborn belong to him. Yet he entered the world to provide for our adoption as sons. Jesus trades places with us, taking on himself the guilt of our sins and paying our penalty, while granting to us the rewards he deserves. This is why we are all adopted as sons (not "children," or, "sons and daughters"). God looks at each of us and sees the righteousness of his Son. He says to each of us what he said to Jesus: "You are my Son. You are the One I love. With you I am well pleased." The ancestors of Jesus acted out this adoption as, again and again, the firstborn was set aside so a brother could receive the blessing, not by law or because of law, but because of grace.

## The sacrifice

Genesis 22 has inspired awe and horror in God's people for many generations. Soren Kierkegaard wrote an entire book, *Fear and Trembling*, about this chapter. He makes the interesting point that any man today who dared to imitate Abraham and prepare to offer his son as a burnt offering would be stopped, arrested, tried, and convicted of a crime. Any statement that God had told him to do such a thing would be disregarded as an attempt to obtain a verdict of innocent on the grounds of insanity.

Kierkegaard overlooked the fact that Genesis 22 contains a picture of Jesus and his sacrifice. However, Kierkegaard correctly indicated that this account teaches more than the truth that we should give our best to God. Many teachers see only that lesson—Isaac was the best thing Abraham could offer to God, and God demanded that from him. A vast distance separates our requirement to give our best to

God and God's command to Abraham to offer his son Isaac as a burnt sacrifice.

How was Abraham capable of daring to obey such a command? "By faith Abraham, when he was tested, offered up Isaac... He considered that God was able even to raise him from the dead, from which, figuratively speaking, he did receive him back" (Hebrews 11:17-18). Abraham's faith in the promise of the resurrection made him able to obey God's command to sacrifice his son. If Abraham knew about the resurrection, he must also have known about the promised Savior. Perhaps Abraham even believed that his miracle son, Isaac, was the promised Savior, the blessing from his family for the entire world. Instead of recognizing Isaac as a picture of Jesus, Abraham may have thought that he was in the presence of his Redeemer in the person of his son.

So a father is prepared to accept—and even to cause—the death of his son for the good of the world. The son trusts his father and does not resist his father's will. He even carries the wood to the place of sacrifice, as Jesus carried his own cross. Abraham is stopped just in time, because Isaac is not the Christ. He is only a picture of the Christ. A second picture of Jesus appears, a ram taking the place of Isaac as Jesus himself would take the place of Isaac in the future.

As they climbed the hill for the sacrifice, Isaac asked Abraham, "Where is the lamb for the burnt offering?" Abraham must have gulped and sighed before he said, "God will provide for himself the lamb for a burnt offering, my son." When he said those words, Abraham expected Isaac to be the lamb, for God had provided Isaac by a miracle to Abraham and Sarah. Abraham's words were made true when he provided a ram caught in a thicket by its horns. They were made more true when God provided his only-begotten Son to be the Lamb of God who takes away the sin of the world.

Not only is Jesus depicted first by Isaac and then by the ram; he is also present at this near-sacrifice. He is the angel of the Lord who speaks to Abraham, repeating the promise that Abraham's family would be a mighty nation and would provide a blessing for the entire world. Jesus himself fulfilled that promise when he suffered and died on the cross and when he rose to life again on the third day. His resurrection guarantees our resurrection and our eternal life. This promise of a resurrection strengthened Abraham to obey the command of God, and (as the letter to the Hebrews says) "figuratively speaking, he did receive him back"—on the third day from the command to sacrifice his son!

Where did this take place? "The land of Moriah... on one of the mountains of which I shall tell you," God said (Genesis 22:2). This mountain of Moriah is mentioned again in II Chronicles 3:1, where we are told that Solomon built the house of the Lord on Mount Moriah. Moriah is one of the seven hills of Jerusalem, and the animal sacrifices (which, like Isaac, were pictures of Jesus) were offered to God in the Temple on Mount Moriah from the time of Solomon until the Babylonian Captivity, and again in the second Temple until the time of Jesus. Calvary may possibly be the very outcropping of Mount Moriah on which Isaac was nearly sacrificed. If not, we can be sure that the place where Father Abraham was prepared to sacrifice his son and the place where God the Father accepted the sacrifice of his Son were very near each other.

## The bride

Isaac is a picture of Christ in at least three ways.
His birth was promised in advance, just as
Moses and the prophets promised the coming
of Christ. Isaac's birth to ninety-year-old Sarah
was a miracle, just as Christ's birth to the virgin
Mary was a miracle. Isaac's father was willing to
sacrifice him for the good of the world, just as
God the Father accepted the sacrifice of his Son
for the good of the world. It stands to reason,
then, that the bride of Isaac should in some way
resemble the Bride of Christ, the Holy Christian
Church.

 Abraham sent a servant to find a wife for his
son Isaac and bring her to him. So also God sent
prophets to prepare the way of the Lord, so
that believers in the coming Savior were
rescued by the same faith in Jesus that rescues
Christians today. The apostles were sent to
make disciples of all nations, and missionaries
are still sent into the world, so that the Church
will consist of people "from every nation, from

84

all tribes and peoples and languages" (Revelation 7:9).

Abraham's servant prayed to God for help. Those who preach and proclaim God's Word do not save sinners by their own words of persuasion. Only Jesus saves sinners; only the Holy Spirit creates saving faith through God's Word. The servant brings the message, but only God can provide the answer.

God answers the servant's prayer "before he had finished speaking" (Genesis 24:15). The timeless God knows what we need and what we will pray. He wants us to pray, to keep in touch with him, but he generously provides for us— even more than what we ask—because of his love for us. Missionaries sometimes find that people who never heard of Jesus or the Christian Church are somehow prepared for the message, coming to faith as soon as they learn of the person and the work of Jesus Christ.

Abraham's servant places jewelry from Abraham upon Rebekah before he speaks to her about marrying Isaac. The members of the Christian Church are not saved from sin and evil by the good things they do for God; they are saved by the good things Jesus has done for them. We bring nothing of our own to be accepted by Jesus as his people; we bring only the works Jesus has done for us—his obedience to his Father's will, his sacrifice on the cross as a Ransom for us, and his victorious resurrection from the dead, defeating all God's enemies on our behalf.

Rebekah is offered no choice whether or not to be married to Isaac. The servant describes his message from Abraham, Laban and Bethuel declare that "the thing has come from the Lord; we cannot speak to you bad or good. Behold, Rebekah is before you, take her and go, and let her be the wife of your master's son, as the Lord has spoken" (Genesis 24:50-51).

Yet after she has been claimed as Isaac's bride, she is given a choice whether she will linger in her old way of life for several days or whether she will leave immediately with Abraham's servant to be brought to Isaac. We cannot choose to come to faith, for we were "dead in the trespasses and sins in which [we] once walked, following the course of this world" (Ephesians 2:1-2). God made us alive, giving us faith—much as the command of Jesus made Lazarus alive and able to walk out of his tomb (John 11:43-44). Being made alive, we can linger in our old sinful ways or live in the new life provided by God's Gospel. The prophets and apostles frequently urge people not to linger in the darkness but to walk in the light. People who are alive have freedom to make good choices or bad choices. People who are dead have no freedom.

Rebekah chooses to travel immediately to her husband, not to linger in her old way of life. So also the Bride of Christ comes to him, to the husband who "might sanctify her, having cleansed her by the washing of water with the Word, so that he might present the Church to himself in splendor, without spot or wrinkle or any such thing, that she might be holy and without blemish" (Ephesians 5:26-27). Once again, Christians do not sanctify themselves for Jesus; they are sanctified by the work of Jesus, done on their behalf.

Before they left her home and her family, Abraham's servant "brought out jewelry of silver and of gold, and garments, and gave them to Rebekah" (Genesis 24:53). When they approached Abraham's home and Rebekah first saw Isaac from a distance, "she took her veil and covered herself" (Genesis 24:65). She came to her husband in clothing that he and his father had already provided to her. As God cast away the fig-leaf clothing Adam and Eve had made and provided suitable clothing for them, so the Church and its members come to Christ clothed in the righteousness he has provided us.

"For as many of you as were baptized into Christ have put on Christ" (Galatians 3:27). Clothed in his righteousness, we are his Church. Today we are still engaged to Christ, waiting for the Bridegroom to come in all his splendor to bring us to his mansion. Already, though, we belong to him, chosen "before the foundation of the world" (Ephesians 1:4) to be his people forever.

## Birthright and blessing

Men like Noah and Abraham are easily seen as pictures of Christ. Though neither man was sinless, they both obeyed the commands of God and brought blessing to the world through their obedience. The account of Esau and Jacob is harder to view in a Christ-centered way. Most often their relationship is treated as a morality play. Jacob cheats his brother and lies to his father; as a result he has to leave home and live with his cousin, Laban, who in turn cheats Jacob in a matter close to Jacob's heart.

What, then, can we say of Esau? Before the twins were born, God declared that "the one shall be stronger than the other, the older shall serve the younger" (Genesis 25:23). Much later God said, "I have loved Jacob, but Esau I have hated" (Malachi 1:2-3). Esau despised his birthright—the blessing he deserved for being Isaac's firstborn son. He exchanged his birthright for a bowl of lentil stew (Genesis 25:29-34). Jacob swindled his brother by offering the exchange, but Esau's low regard for his birthright seems to disqualify Esau as a picture of Christ.

Yet at least Esau got a bowl of soup in exchange for his birthright. Jesus Christ is the only-begotten Son of God. He lived a sinless life worthy of great rewards. Yet he exchanged all that belonged to him and all that he deserved. He surrendered it all to take on himself the burden of our sins. We are adopted into the family of God by this exchange, and all our guilt is removed from our lives. Instead of a bowl of soup, Jesus receives a cross of suffering. He is abandoned by his Father—which we deserve for our sins—and yet he prays for sinners, "Father, forgive them, for they know not what they do" (Luke 23:34).

Even though Esau had surrendered his birthright to Jacob, and in spite of the fact that God had foretold Jacob's success over Esau, Isaac still stubbornly wanted to bless his firstborn son. He sent Esau on a hunting expedition, and Esau went out into the wilderness in obedience to his father's command. At this time, Isaac's bride Rebekah enters the picture. She plans the deception of Isaac and performs all the work. She cooks the kids, she makes the goatskin gloves for Jacob to wear, and she dresses him in Esau's clothing. Isaac is blind to his son's deception, as God the Father is blind in love, accepting us in the name of his Son. As the Church by its teaching and by its blessings clothes us in the righteousness of Christ to bring us to God the Father, so Jacob is prepared by his mother to receive his father's blessing, the blessing Isaac wanted to give to the son who was doing what Isaac told him to do.

Jacob nearly ruins the scheme by fumbling his one task—when he speaks to his father, he forgets to imitate his brother's voice. Yet, being blind, Isaac trusts his senses of touch and taste and smell over his sense of hearing. He grants to Jacob the blessing he wanted to give to Esau.

He treats Jacob as the son who is doing his father's will. The same thing happens to Christians today, as God the Father says of Christians what he said to Jesus on the day Jesus was baptized: "You are my Son. You are the one I love. With you I am well-pleased."

## Jacob's ladder

When Jacob had deceived his father and claimed his brother's blessing, he had to run away from home. Jesus willingly gives to Christians the reward that Jesus deserved for obeying his father's will, but Esau plots to kill his brother Jacob. Rebekah sends Jacob to her family, a place of safety, until enough time has passed that Esau will have lost his anger.

His first night away from home, Jacob meets Jesus. He takes a stone for his pillow and lays down to sleep. "And he dreamed, and behold, there was a ladder set up on the earth, and the top of it reached to heaven. And behold, the angels of God were ascending and descending on it" (Genesis 28:12). Jesus stood above the ladder and spoke to Jacob, renewing the promise he had made to Abraham and Isaac. The same triple blessing is spoken: Jacob's family will become a mighty nation, they will live on the land where Jacob was sleeping, and through that family on that land all the nations of the world will be blessed. (Again, the promise spoken by Jesus to Jacob is the promise fulfilled by Jesus when he comes to obey his Father and to sacrifice himself on a cross so our sins can be forgiven and we can be welcomed into the Kingdom of God.)

Jacob takes this dream to indicate that he has been sleeping in the house of God and at the gate of heaven (Genesis 28:17). He sets up a landmark to remember the place. Then he does what sinners so often do: he tries to bargain with God. Although God has made unconditional promises to Jacob, Jacob offers God a deal—if God will keep his promise to take care of Jacob, then the Lord will be Jacob's God and the landmark Jacob made will be God's house. Moreover, Jacob promises God one-tenth of Jacob's wealth. God did not ask for any of this. He blessed Jacob because God's nature is to love, to bless, and to show mercy. God's plan, as described in his promise, is much bigger than the fortunes of Jacob. Yet Jacob takes this promise personally, thinking only of what's in this promise for Jacob.

Not only did Jacob see Jesus at the top of the ladder; in the ladder itself he saw a picture of Jesus. We know this because of the words of Jesus: "Truly, truly, I say to you, you will see heaven opened, and the angels of God ascending and descending on the Son of Man" (John 1:51). Jesus is the only Way to the Father, the only way from this sinful earth to God's perfect new creation. Jesus is the ladder, although if escalators had been invented when the book of Genesis was written, they would have been an even better picture of Jesus, bearing us up to heaven at no effort to ourselves.

Wrestling with God, and the face of God

Jacob lived with his cousin Laban and married Laban's daughters. He gained a large family and became a wealthy man with large flocks and herds of livestock. The time finally came for Jacob to return home. He tried to slip away from Laban with his family and his livestock, but Laban pursued Jacob. Jesus personally warned Laban neither to bless nor curse Jacob. So the two men created a monument to mark a border between their two families, and they promised to leave each other alone.

Jacob was afraid that Esau would still be angry with Jacob. As Jacob once tried to bargain with God, now he tried to buy his brother's love and forgiveness. He sent hundreds of animals ahead of him, telling the servants driving those animals that they were a present for Esau. Jacob even thought, "I may appease him with the present that goes ahead of me, and afterward I shall see his face. Perhaps he will accept me" (Genesis 32:20). Jacob then sent his family and his remaining possessions across the stream and prepared to spend the night alone.

Jacob was not alone that night. Instead, he wrestled with a man until daybreak. Although the man showed that he had the power to dislocate Jacob's bones with just a touch, the man treated Jacob as an equal and did not defeat him. This man then changed Jacob's name to Israel, saying, "You have striven with God and with men, and have prevailed" (Genesis 32:28). When Jacob asked, his opponent refused to tell Jacob his name. Jacob knew the identity of his opponent, though, because he named the place Peniel, saying, "I have seen God face to face, and yet my life has been delivered" (Genesis 32:30).

Jacob knew that he had just had a close encounter with God. Since "no one has ever seen God; the only God who is at the Father's side he has made him known" (John 1:18), we can be confident that the wrestling partner of Jacob was Jesus. Why wouldn't Jesus tell Jacob his name? To know someone's name is to have power over that person. Even after wrestling Jesus to a draw, Jacob could not have power over Jesus. Despite all his attempts to bargain with God (and with his brother Esau), Jacob was still powerless—he had to trust God to keep God's promises. So, in the last book of the Bible, it says that Jesus "has a name written that no one knows but himself" (Revelation 19:12). What is the use of a name that no one else knows? It shows that no one else has power over Jesus.

While some people describe the body of Jacob's wrestling partner as the "pre-incarnate Christ," a special miracle body for that one wrestling match, I maintain that Jacob wrestled with Jesus, who was in his own true body. This body of Jesus had been conceived within the virgin Mary, born in Bethlehem, and raised in Nazareth. In that body he preached and taught, he gathered disciples, and he worked miracles. In that body he was arrested, beaten, mocked, scourged, and crucified. That body was buried in Jerusalem, raised on the third day, and ascended into heaven. At his ascension, Jesus filled all things (Ephesians 4:10), time as well as space. Because Jesus is God, he has the ability to leave time and space and enter them elsewhere, without needing a DeLorean or a Tardis. Jacob wrestled with the body of his Savior, a body which bore the scars of nails on his hands and on his feet.

After wrestling with Jesus, Jacob met his brother Esau. Esau forgave Jacob his sins and refused to accept his gifts. He ran to meet Jacob and embraced him, much like the father in the parable of the Prodigal Son. When Esau tried to return Jacob's animals, Jacob said, "No, please, if I have found favor in your sight, then accept my present from my hand. For I have seen your face, which is like seeing the face of God, and you have accepted me" (Genesis 33:10).

Jacob had seen Jesus face to face and had wrestled with him. He even said, "I have seen

God face to face, and yet my life has been delivered." Now Jacob says to Esau, "I have seen your face, which is like seeing the face of God." For Jacob, Esau was a picture of Jesus. Can he be any less for us?

Esau did not need gifts from Jacob, but out of kindness he accepted his brother's gifts. God needs nothing from us, but out of grace he accepts our gifts. Not only the money we give to the Church, but also the good deeds we do for our neighbors, are gifts to Jesus. Jesus takes personally the things we do for people in need (Matthew 2534-40). Yet his love and his forgiveness do not depend upon what we do, for they have already been granted to us.

## Joseph and bros.

Jacob begat twelve sons and at least one daughter. They were conceived by Jacob's two wives, sisters Leah and Rachel, and by the servants of each of those wives. Jacob's favorite wife was Rachel, and her firstborn son was Joseph. To show his preference for Joseph, Jacob gave him a formal garment, usually described in English as "a coat of many colors."

Like Jesus, Joseph was the son who was favored by his father. Like Jesus, Joseph was hated because of the special relationship he had with his father. Joseph's own brothers rejected him, as Jesus' own people rejected him. While Joseph was obeying the will of his father, his brothers seized him violently and plotted his death. They ended up selling him for a certain number of pieces of silver (twenty, not thirty). Before they did so, however, they threw him into a pit in the ground, not intending to bring him out alive again. In this way, Joseph acted out the death and burial of Jesus, as well as his rejection and betrayal from his own people.

The picture of Christ in the life of Joseph becomes even clearer because of his formal garment. When his brothers seized Joseph, they stripped him of his coat of many colors. To deceive their father, they stained the coat with animal blood and brought it to their father. They claimed to have found it in a field, and their phony concern for their brother was expressed in terms of, "We hope nothing bad happened to poor little Joe." Jacob believed the evidence of his son's death. He accepted the sons who brought him evidence of Joseph's death, little realizing that they had, in fact, plotted that death and only narrowly turned aside from killing Joseph.

As Isaac was deceived by Jacob because Jacob was wearing Esau's clothing, so Jacob is deceived by his sons because of the clothing they bring to him. As Christians, we approach our heavenly Father wearing the righteousness of Jesus. We are not holy. We are not worthy of God's approval. We do not deserve to approach him at all, let alone be claimed by him as sons. Yet, because we come to the Father clothed in Christ's righteousness, he accepts us. He calls us his children, says that he loves us, and declares that he is well pleased with us.

The garment we bring to our Father is also stained with blood. Jesus died a bloody death to take away our sins. Our heavenly Father claims us, not only because of the righteousness of Christ, but also because of the blood of Christ. Animals once represented Christ on the altars of the Old Testament, as an animal shed its blood to take the place of Joseph. Now that Jesus has suffered and died, we no longer sacrifice animals to God. Jesus is the ultimate sacrifice of which all the bulls and lambs and goats of the Old Testament Law were pictures.

Meanwhile, as a slave in Egypt, Joseph suffered further indignities. He did the will of his master and did not fall short of expectations, yet he became the victim of a lie. Potiphar's wife claimed that Joseph attacked her and tried to rape her, when the truth was that she had tried to seduce Joseph. Once again, Joseph's clothing was presented as evidence, this time condemning him to punishment he did not deserve. Joseph suffered in Egypt while doing the right thing, just as Jesus suffered on the cross while doing the right thing. Both were sentenced by Gentile governments, yet in the end both prevailed in time over those same governments. After a few years, Joseph was running Egypt. After about three hundred years, Christianity became the official religion of the Roman Empire.

## At the right hand

Throughout history, certain kings and emperors and other executive authorities have enjoyed the privilege of rule without accepting any of the responsibility of rule. Sometimes they were considered too important to do the work of government. Sometimes they were incompetent. Sometimes they were merely lazy. In every case, someone else was found to do the real work of governing the land. Joseph became such a man in Egypt. After interpreting the dreams of Pharaoh, predicting seven years of bounty followed by seven years of famine, Joseph was put in charge of Egypt, collecting supplies during the good times to take care of people during the bad times. Joseph ran Egypt, while the Pharaoh sat on the throne and enjoyed the worship of his people. In a similar way, in the book of Esther, first Haman and then Mordecai took royal authority in Persia. The real emperor sat on the throne, but his prime ministers did the work of running the empire.

We call such a power a "right hand man." As the right hand of the king or emperor, he does the work to run the country while the chief executive gets the credit. Medieval France had a "mayor of the palace" doing the real work while the Merovingian kings got all the credit. Medieval Japan had a Shogun doing the real work while the Japanese emperors got all the credit. Modern corporations and universities often have a President who receives all the credit while a presidential assistant is doing the real work that brings success to the business.

After his resurrection, Jesus told his apostles, "All power in heaven and on earth has been given to me" (Matthew 28:18). The apostle Paul shared the same message in a different way, saying that Jesus is seated at the right hand of God the Father (Ephesians 1:20 and Colossians 3:1, among others). The right hand of the Father is not a ceremonial position. Sitting at the

Father's right hand means doing the work of the Father. Because Jesus has been given power and authority by the Father, Jesus is the only Way to approach the Father. Those who try to come to God the Father through their own good deeds, or because they were created by him, cannot reach the Father. Only through Christ can the Father be approached.

As the Pharaoh's right-hand man, Joseph had power to reward people and power to punish people. Though they did not recognize Joseph, his brothers placed themselves under his power when they came to buy food in Egypt. Joseph, unlike Jesus, was not sinless. He could not resist the temptation to toy with his brothers before he finally told them who he was. Like Christ, though, Joseph forgave his brothers all their sins against him. He provided generously for his family without accepting any payment from them. In the end, he brought them to live with him, as Jesus brings his people into Paradise and into the new creation. Our sins caused

Jesus to suffer, as the sins of his brothers caused Joseph to suffer. Yet Jesus does not hold a grudge against any of us. He forgives us, he provides for us now, and he has guaranteed us a home where we will live with him forever in peace and joy.

## The Lion of the tribe of Judah

Before he died, Jacob gathered his sons and prophesied about their future. Beginning with the oldest, he worked his way through each son, speaking of what would happen to their families. His longest blessing was reserved for Judah, the son through whom the messianic promised to Abraham, Isaac, and Jacob would be fulfilled.

Jacob began by saying that Judah's brothers would praise him and that his father's sons would bow down before him. At this time, such statements would have been more appropriate to describe Joseph, who was running Egypt and was using his authority to take care of his family. When the children of Israel returned to the Promised Land and defeated the Canaanites, the tribes of Ephraim and Manasseh (descended from Joseph) dominated northern Israel while the tribe of Judah dominated in the south. The first king, Saul, came from the tribe of Benjamin, but the most successful dynasty of Israel was that of David, who came from the tribe of Judah.

Jacob spoke of that dynasty and of the messianic King who would come from David's family. "Judah is a lion's cub," Jacob said. "From the prey, my son, you have gone up. He stooped down; he crouched as a lion and as a lioness; who dares rouse him?" Revelation 5:5 associates Jesus with this verse, saying, "Behold: the Lion of the tribe of Judah, the Root of David, has conquered, so that he can open the scroll and its seven seals." Satan is also called a lion in the Bible, though he is more often connected with a serpent, the form he chose to use to deceive Eve. Yet Jesus is also represented by a serpent in Numbers 21, as Jesus himself affirms in John 3:14-15.

"The scepter shall not depart from Judah, nor the ruler's staff from between his feet, until Shiloh comes," Jacob said. Commentaries on Genesis devote pages to deciphering the identity of Shiloh. A city of this name was built and for a time was home to the Tabernacle, but the city was probably named for the promise, rather than the promise predicting the city. "Shiloh" appears related to "Shalom," which means peace, and some interpreters have suggested that the promise was fulfilled with Solomon, the son of David. Yet the best interpretation of this verse is that Shiloh is another name for the Messiah, the Prince of Peace. Solomon was only another picture of Jesus, but Jesus himself is the fulfillment of this promise. When Roman authority placed Herod, the Idumean, over the Jews, then it was time for the true King of the Jews to be born.

"To him shall be the obedience of the peoples. Binding his foal to the vine and his donkey's colt to the choice vine, he has washed his garments in wine and his vesture in the blood of grapes. His eyes are darker than wine, and his teeth whiter than milk." All these images are fulfilled in Jesus. He rode a colt, the foal of a donkey, into Jerusalem. He declared to his followers, "I am the Vine, and you are the branches." He shed his blood on the cross to rescue sinners, but a few hours earlier he held a cup of wine in his hands and said, "This cup that is poured out for you is the new testament in my blood" (Luke 22:20). Before he died, his own clothing was taken away by the soldiers; but through his death, Jesus has clothed his people in his righteousness. As Adam and Eve were clothed by God, and as Jacob was accepted by Isaac because of Esau's clothing, and as the brothers of Joseph brought the blood-stained robe of Joseph to their father, so we are clothed in Christ, washed clean in his blood, and made acceptable to our Father.

By his prophecy, Jacob prepared his family for the coming of the Messiah. Jesus is the Son of David, the Prince of Peace, the Redeemer of the world. He is the Lion of the tribe of Judah, set to rule all nations under his scepter and to bring peace to the entire world.

"Am I in the place of God?"

After Jacob died, his sons feared that Joseph may have been delaying his vengeance until that time. Their guilty consciences made it hard for them to believe that Joseph sincerely and whole-heartedly forgave their sins. Therefore, they sent a message to Joseph. They claimed that, before he died, Jacob had demanded forgiveness from Joseph for his brothers. We cannot tell whether or not Jacob said such a thing. No record of Jacob's message about forgiveness appears in Genesis, aside from the quote given by Joseph's brothers. Their guilt and fear may have tempted them into lying to their brother. It did not matter, though, because Joseph had already forgiven his brothers all their sins.

Before he died, Jesus commanded his followers to forgive those who sin against us. He even put into his model prayer a promise to forgive those who sin against us. Jesus spoke so firmly about forgiveness that some Christians believe that forgiving those who hurt us is a requirement for salvation. They think that the Bible says that we must forgive first so that God will forgive us. They forget that God always goes first. We forgive others only because of the forgiveness of God. We forgive others, passing along the forgiveness won by Jesus on the cross. Refusing to forgive someone who has hurt us calls God's complete forgiveness into question. If a sin against us is too big for God to forgive, how can we be sure that he has forgiven all our sins? But we do not forgive sinners out of the goodness of our hearts. We forgive sinners because Jesus has already purchased their forgiveness by his blood, his suffering, and his death.

Why does God allow sins to happen, knowing that we will be hurt by the sins of others? In the abstract, Christians can find answers to that question. Dealing with a specific sin, we do not always know which answer applies. In the case of Joseph, he was allowed to know the answer to that question. In Genesis 50:20, Joseph reports, "You intended it for evil, but God intended it for good, so that many people are alive today." God permitted the sin of Joseph's brothers so Joseph could sit at the right hand of Pharaoh and run Egypt, saving the lives of the Egyptian people and of their neighbors, including Joseph's family.

Sometime God allows sin and evil so we can see the true nature of sin and evil and reject them, preferring what is good. Sometimes God allows sin and evil because he has a way of turning them into a greater blessing, as he did in the case of Joseph. Sometimes God allows sin and evil to provide an opportunity for his people to do good things, forgiving the sinner and helping the victims of sin. Sometimes God allows sin and evil to remind his people of the suffering of Christ on the cross. The devil persecutes God's people, intended to make us doubt God's goodness or love or power. When our troubles remind us how God saved us through the suffering of his Son, the devil is thwarted and God's Kingdom remains victorious.

God does not cause evil, although even evil things come from his creation. Evil is not equal to good; evil is good that has been twisted and misused. God placed metal in the ground and gave skill to a craftsman who makes a knife from that metal. When that knife is used in a murder, God is not at fault. He permitted that sin for a reason, and he provided the ways that sin could take place. If he allowed that sin and did not intervene to prevent that sin (and only God knows how many times he has intervened to prevent evil), then he had a reason to allow that sin. God is under no obligation to tell us all his reasons.

"Am I in the place of God?" Joseph asked his brothers when they came to Joseph looking for forgiveness. The way he phrased the question, he expected the answer to be "no." Yet as a picture of Christ, his forgiveness was Christ's forgiveness. He had authority to punish his brothers or to forgive them. He was indeed in the place of God, and his forgiveness was a vivid picture of God's forgiveness given freely to sinners.

When Peter declared his faith that Jesus is the Christ, the Son of God, Jesus congratulated Peter on that declaration and added, "I give you the keys to the kingdom of heaven. Whatever you unlock on earth is unlocked in heaven, and whatever you lock on earth is locked in heaven" (Matthew 16:16-19). Later, Jesus said the same words to all his apostles (Matthew 18:18). After he had died and had risen from the dead, Jesus said the same thing a third time. John says that Jesus breathed on the apostles and said, "Receive the Holy Spirit. Whatever you forgive on earth is forgiven in heaven, and whatever you do not forgive on earth is not forgiven in heaven" (John 20:22-23).

Who has the keys to heaven? Who has the power to forgive sins (or to withhold forgiveness)? Everyone who has received the

Holy Spirit has this power. Since we know that "no one can say Jesus is Lord apart from the Holy Spirit" (I Corinthians 12:3), everyone who confesses faith in Jesus has the power to forgive sins. Everyone who, like Peter, knows that Jesus is the Christ, the Son of God, is able to share his forgiveness with sinners.

Why would Jesus also give the power to lock heaven, to refuse forgiveness to sinners? He tells us not to give dogs what is holy and not to cast pearls before swine (Matthew 7:6). We do not speak words of forgiveness to people who boast of their sins, who refuse to admit that what they are doing is wrong, who do not want to be forgiven. God calls sinners to repent. Because we have the keys to heaven, we also call sinners to repent. Our goal is always to lead sinners to repent so we can forgive them. Yet our words of forgiveness would have no meaning if we said them to everyone, even to sinners who proudly continue to sin and who do not care whether or not God has forgiven them.

"Am I in the place of God?" Since he was a picture of the Christ, Joseph should have been answered "yes." "Am I in the place of God?" Jesus says, "Yes, you are." He could bring forgiveness to sinners any way he chose. After purchasing full forgiveness on the cross, Jesus chose to bring forgiveness to sinners through the work of his Church. Every member of that Church has the power to share Christ's forgiveness. Every person on earth is either a missionary or a mission opportunity.

Like Adam, like Abel, like Abraham and Isaac and Esau, Joseph was a picture of Christ. Today, in a different way, every Christian is a picture of Christ. (That is why we are called Christians.) God wanted ancient people to know his plan of salvation, and he wants people today to know the same plan. He chooses to work with us--his will be done.

62052920R00068

Made in the USA
Lexington, KY
28 March 2017